Contents

The dinosaurs

Dinosaurs were reptiles.

Dinosaurs

Brachiosaurus

Daniel Nunn

www.heinemann.co.uk/library
Visit our website to find out more information about Heinemann Library books.

To order:
☎ Phone 44 (0) 1865 888066
  Send a fax to 44 (0) 1865 314091
📄 Visit the Heinemann Bookshop at www.heinemann.co.uk/library to browse our
💻 catalogue and order online.

First published in Great Britain by Heinemann Library,
Halley Court, Jordan Hill, Oxford OX2 8EJ, part of Harcourt
Education. Heinemann is a registered trademark of Harcourt
Education Ltd.

© Harcourt Education Ltd 2007
First published in paperback in 2008
The moral right of the proprietor has been asserted.

ABERDEENSHIRE LIBRARY AND	
INFORMATION SERVICES	
2613037	
HJ	646125
J567.91	£5.25
JU	JNF

Printed and bound in China by South China
Printing Co. Ltd.

10 digit ISBN 0 431 18450 X (hardback)
13 digit ISBN 978 0431 184500 (hardback)

11 10 09 08 07
10 9 8 7 6 5 4 3 2 1

10 digit ISBN 0 431 18457 7 (paperback)
13 digit ISBN 978 0431 184579 (paperback)

12 11 10 09 08
10 9 8 7 6 5 4 3 2 1

British Library Cataloguing in Publication Data
Nunn, Daniel
Brachiosaurus. – (Dinosaurs)
567.9'12
A full catalogue record for this book is available from the
British Library

Acknowledgements
The publishers would like to thank the following for permission
to reproduce photographs: Alamy pp. 6, 10 and 23 (Mike
Danton), 22 (www.white-windmill.co.uk); Corbis pp. 7
(Galen Rowell), 12 (Jim Zuckerman), 22 (Louie Psihoyos);
Getty images pp. 18 (National Geographic/Maria Stenzel),
19 (Science Faction/Louie Psihoyos), 20 and 23 (The Image
Bank/Grant Faint), 21 (News/Cancan Chu).

Cover photograph of Brachiosaurus reproduced with
permission of Corbis/Jim Zuckerman.

Every effort has been made to contact copyright holders
of any material reproduced in this book. Any omissions will
be rectified in subsequent printings if notice is given to the
publishers.

Dinosaurs lived long ago.

Brachiosaurus was a dinosaur.

Brachiosaurus lived long ago.

Today there are no Brachiosaurus.

Brachiosaurus

Compsognathus

Some dinosaurs were small.

But Brachiosaurus was very big.

Brachiosaurus had long legs.

Brachiosaurus walked slowly.

Brachiosaurus had a very long neck.

Brachiosaurus could eat the
leaves at the top of trees.

Brachiosaurus ate plants.

Brachiosaurus ate stones, too!

Sometimes, other dinosaurs
attacked Brachiosaurus.

Brachiosaurus used its feet to fight back.

How do we know?

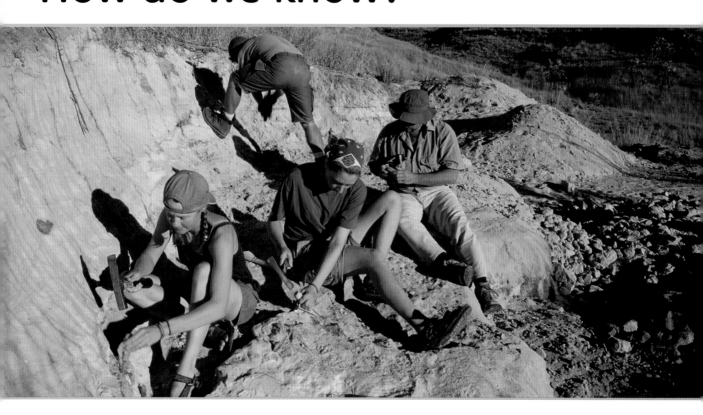

Scientists have found fossils
of Brachiosaurus.

Fossils are the bones of animals
which have turned to rock.

fossil

Fossils show us the outline of the dinosaur.

Fossils tell us what
Brachiosaurus was like.

Fossil quiz

A

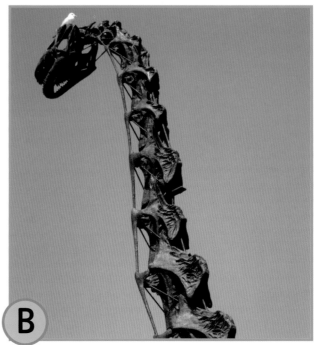

B

One of these fossils was Brachiosaurus.
Can you tell which one?

Picture glossary

dinosaur a reptile who lived millions of years ago

fossil part of a dead plant or animal that has become hard like rock

reptile a cold-blooded animal

Answer to question on page 22
Fossil B was Brachiosaurus. Fossil A was Triceratops.

Index

Notes to Parents and Teachers
Before reading
Talk to the children about dinosaurs. Do they know the names of any dinosaurs?
What features did they have e.g. long neck, bony plates, sharp teeth? Has anyone
seen a dinosaur fossil or model in a museum?

After reading
• Sing a Dinosaur song to the tune of 'London Bridge is falling down'.
  Dinosaurs lived long ago, long ago, long ago.
  Dinosaurs lived long ago
  Now they are extinct.
  Continue with e.g. Brachiosaurus had a very long neck/ Brachiosaurus ate plants
  and stones etc.
• Read a dinosaur story e.g. *Dinosaur Roar* by Paul and Henrietta Strickland
• Make a Brachiosaurus collage. Draw a large outline of a Brachiosaurus and help
  the children cover the body using scrunched tissue paper etc.